The Real
And Only Life

The Real
And Only Life

by Nancy Peerman

Introduction by Keith Miller

WORD BOOKS

WACO, TEXAS

Grateful acknowledgement is made to the following for permission to use copyright material:

THE DIVISION OF CHRISTIAN EDUCATION OF THE NATIONAL COUNCIL OF THE CHURCHES OF CHRIST IN THE U.S.A.
  Quotations from the Revised Standard Version of The Bible. copyright © 1948 and 1952. Used by permission
THE MACMILLAN COMPANY
  Quotations from *The New Testament in Modern English* by J. B. Phillips, copyright © 1958. Used by permission
ZONDERVAN PUBLISHING HOUSE
  A quotation from *The Amplified Old Testament*, Part Two, Copyright © 1962
THE ALFRED A. KNOPF COMPANY
  Quotations from *The Prophet* by Kahlil Gibran, copyright 1923, 1951.

Printed in The United States of America

PREFACE   □

There are many questions being asked today about religion. People have always needed answers and looked for what was real in the midst of confusion, but in our present world the need seems more acute. I know it was for me.

For a long time I think I was asking the wrong question. While I talked about religion, what I was really interested in was life—my life; how to live it, what it meant, how to find peace and joy in spite of the problems that were part of living.

It is for people like myself that I have written this book.

ACKNOWLEDGEMENTS □

In my life there have been many important people. Certainly my mother and my father were the first of many who influenced the direction in which I have gone. I owe my thanks to so very many people, some of whom do not know how much they have given me. The sum of my life includes all of them.

I am particularly thankful for four good friends—Barbara Dan and Howard Butt, and Mary Allen and Keith Miller. Each of them has offered me encouragement, advice, and help in writing this book, and beyond that they have played a part in helping me live out what this book is all about.

But there is one person to whom I am especially grateful for encouragement. He urged me to try what I was certain I could not do. It is to him, my friend and my husband, that this book is dedicated.

Nancy Peerman
Corpus Christi, Texas

INTRODUCTION

☐

This story really happened to some dear friends. I have seen some of it take place. When I first met Bob and Nancy Peerman at a weekend Christian conference several years ago, I picked them out of a group of about forty-five people as the couple seeming the least likely to be interested in a deeply committed Christian life. Bob was openly cynical and Nancy appeared to be very aloof. But since that time the things which have happened in and through their lives have been a great source of inspiration and strength to me in my own struggles to find God's will.

Whenever couples tell me they are bored, restless, and dissatisfied with life—even though they have health and friends and are making a good living—I remember the Peermans and the miracle of newness God has brought into their lives. And when I am asked by cynical churchmen how they might begin motivating their people toward catching a vision of the reality of the Living God for modern suburbanites, I often suggest that they ask Bob and Nancy to come and tell part of the story you are about to read.

To write simply and directly without preaching at the reader is a very difficult thing to do, and I think Nancy has done it. She has let us look through her eyes at a new experience of living which she is discovering as a wife, mother, and friend in a world from which she once hid behind a mask of sophistication.

This is an authentic Christian witness and I believe it will help thousands of people to find new direction toward a life which is "really real."

KEITH MILLER
Austin, Texas

CONTENTS ☐

Follow the river and you will find the sea.
A French Proverb

CHAPTER 1

CHAPTER 1

A QUESTION OF LIFE

"God's not interested in my life. He's far too busy being God!" I felt very sure of what I was saying; what I couldn't figure out was how my doctor and I had gotten on the subject of God. I'd come in to see him because I was feeling rundown and nervous. I had asked him what was wrong with me, and now we were talking about God.

"Who do you think God is, Nancy?" He said it quietly, but my anger flared just the same. He was an Episcopalian, just as I was—in fact we were members of the same church. He ought to know what I believed. I felt he was questioning my faith and I resented it.

"Well, He's the Creator and He's all-powerful. He's to be worshipped. He's . . . well, He's God! Why did you ask me about God?"

"You and I both know that your problems aren't really physical. I think it's time we were honest with each other."

I knew that he wanted to help me, but I couldn't be honest,

and I was afraid to admit, even to myself, some of the things that were bothering me. Our conversation ended politely but quickly and I left his office. But I could not shake off the question that he had raised.

I had always accepted the fact that there was a God. As a little girl of eight I began attending an Episcopal church with my best friend who was a member there. I was a shy child, perhaps because I had no brothers or sisters, and I was a little bit afraid of people. I wasn't afraid in church, though; I felt at home there, and I thought it was a beautiful place. It offered me security during those years, and I gladly accepted its teachings about a God who was Father, Son and Holy Ghost. I wasn't sure that I understood it all, but I loved the church so I did not question what I was taught. I grew up singing in the choir, going to Sunday school and participating in all the activities for young people.

At the age of sixteen I went off to college in a large city and found there a wider world than my hometown of Corpus Christi. People were still frightening to me, but by this time I had learned to hide my fears behind a mask of doing and saying the right thing. I soon learned how naive I was. In the name of sophistication I quickly adopted new standards and became part of the social set that centered around sororities—I tried to fit in with the crowd. My freshman roomate was a very bright girl who sensed some of my uncertainties. One night when we were talking she said, "Nancy, you remind me of a walled garden. I know that there must be something inside the wall you've put around yourself, but all I can do is peek over it occasionally. You just won't let anyone in." Although I denied it, I knew she was right.

I continued my church life by joining an Episcopal group on campus, but much of what I had accepted of the Church's teachings was being called into question by the expansion of my mind in the classroom setting. A question posed to us as students in philosophy class was this—"If God is all good and this is

His world, how do you explain the presence of evil in the world?" I don't remember how I answered the question at the time, but I do remember that question. As a typical college student in revolt against the established order of things, I was very conscious of injustice and suffering in the world. In addition, I was aware that there was something wrong with me and my relationships with other people.

In spite of the sense of wrongness that I had about myself I carried on a normal college life. I played the dating game, studied, and talked all night with friends about the great questions of life. My junior year was a very social one; at home I was formally introduced to society. "Coming out" was fun, but at first the parties were something of an ordeal, because I had to say the right thing to the right person, whether he was a college senior or somebody's grandfather. Soon, though, my image was properly polished and I could hold my own in almost any situation. It was at one of the parties that I met Bob Peerman, who seemed like Prince Charming to me. He was tall and handsome, and he had a promising future designing and building homes. Our courtship was breathless, and I was overwhelmed with my good fortune when he asked me to marry him. We had a large and beautiful church wedding, and I was sure that this was going to be the "live happily ever after" part of my life, for I was in love with him and he was in love with me.

What bothered me, though, was the suspicion that he did not know the real me, for I had carefully hidden from him some of my fears and my sense of loneliness. I felt that he expected his wife to be a poised young lady who could cope with everything. Setting out to be the perfect wife, I molded myself into what I thought my husband wanted. It soon became apparent to me that however wonderful marriage was, it didn't solve the problems one brought down the aisle. Having assumed the role of perfect wife I didn't want Bob to see me out of character, and although it was hard work I managed to please him most of the time. The complexities of a close relationship were hard for me to deal with, but I played a good game.

Several years after Bob and I were married, our first son was born. I had anticipated that motherhood would be a time of fulfillment for me, but it was a real shock when the nurse brought me our little boy and I realized that I had to take him home, that he was my responsibility. Never having been around babies much I honestly didn't know what you did with them. In time I learned to be a mother, but it wasn't quite as fulfilling as I had anticipated. Taking care of a baby was a lot of work and when our second boy was born two years later, I decided that I was not really the motherly type. Although I loved my children, I began to look beyond my home to find what was missing in my life. Involvement in many civic and social affairs came easy and I was busy from morning to night.

God did not enter into my thinking very much after I became an adult. Questions about religion were put out of my mind because I was busily involved with the business of living. Bob was not interested in the church, although he had become an Episcopalian after our marriage. We maintained our membership, saw to it that our children were baptized and were taken to Sunday school. But for Bob and me the vital part of life seemed to be in the business and social world, not in the religious world.

We were beginning to be successful in terms of what the world had to offer. We were young, we had money, and we were in a comfortable position socially. Our marriage was better than average, and we had two nice children. Bob was satisfied with our life, but for me something was missing. I was restless, vaguely disenchanted—I lived from one excitement to another but in between I was terribly bored.

For one thing, it required a lot of effort to keep up the front I had created for myself. I was tired of my roles and images, and it became increasingly hard to play the perfect wife, the good mother, the active club-woman, the polished hostess. Not one of these roles was the real me, and the weight of them was depressing. It was at this point that I went to my doctor. I suppose I hoped that he'd find something wrong with me physically to explain my unhappiness, but instead, he had talked to me in terms of my problems and how God could help.

Here I was twenty-eight, surrounded by all the things in life I had dreamed of having, yet I wasn't happy. It didn't make sense, but there it was. Life was a disappointment, and I didn't know what to do about it. I threw myself into an even busier whirl, but I was steadily more depressed. It was as though I'd pulled a thread and the fabric of my life was beginning to unravel and come apart, and I began to be very much afraid of what was happening to me.

Save me, O God!
For the waters have come up to my neck.
I sink in deep mire,
where there is no foothold . . .

Psalms 69:1, 2 (RSV)

CHAPTER 2

Chapter 2

Who Can Stand Alone?

The struggle did not end easily. In retrospect I see my life at that time as a series of pitched battles, most of them lost. I searched for something to give meaning to my life, for something that could be relied on. The inability to be honest in my relationships with other people seemed to be my biggest problem. I was afraid they wouldn't like me if they saw me as I really was. This lack of reality in my relationships with others was a growing frustration, but I couldn't seem to change.

I did discover that a Martini could dull my sense of isolation, and that a tranquilizer helped put off until tomorrow what I didn't want to face today. I was careful to be appropriate about my drinking, and for the most part I kept it in the context of social occasions. In the crowd we partied with no one cared how much you drank as long as you didn't get embarrassing about it, but I began creating an increasing number of new occasions to drink. Gradually, between the Martinis and the Miltown I was aenaesthetized most of the time. Deep down inside I knew that this was a deadly game, that alcohol and pills were a bad combination, but this knowledge didn't even slow me down.

The situation got worse and worse. Finally in desperation I went to see a psychiatrist. At first he puzzled me because he wouldn't tell me what my problem was and he refused to prescribe any solutions. Rather, we explored my reactions, my fears, my mixed emotions about people. It soon became clear that I was a dependent person and always used other human beings for support. There was something within me that needed "to cling," and I put my trust in first one person and then another, transfering allegiance if one of my idols failed me. It seemed impossible for me to stand alone. Having outgrown the physical dependence of childhood, my childish emotional needs had remained.

It was not hard to trace the thread of my dependence. My father was the strong figure in my younger years, for I was his only child, born late in his life, and he lavished love and interest on me to an unusual degree. He had an inquiring mind, a keen sense of ethics, sympathy for the underdog and a conviction that one day the world was going to be a better place through the efforts of man. He was well educated and was vitally interested in the development of my mind. But his excessive attention and concern had produced a precocious little girl whose emotional maturity lagged behind that of her mind. I adored him, but the measure of my love was also the measure of my disappointment as I began to see his shortcomings. I wanted him to be perfect.

When I married Bob I did not lose a god; I just acquired a second one. My husband was strong of will, decisive, a sturdy support, but he could not always sustain the weight of being responsible for my happiness. I leaned on father and husband, but neither proved to be entirely dependable, not because they wouldn't but because they couldn't. In demanding too much of them as human beings, I became disillusioned when they did not meet my demands. Still I sought from others the love and support that I had to have, and I bought that love with my desire to please. I sold myself in bondage to the wishes of others, for nothing was as important to me as the esteem of those who peopled my world.

I knew well the frustration of trying to please, and I worked very hard to keep myself in everyone's good graces, but it was impossible to get all my dependent relationships working right. People did not react in a consistent way; the important figures in my life did not always play their roles the way I had planned. They did things that were weak and foolish and displayed tendencies that were not admirable by *my* standards.

These feelings became recognizable in the sessions with the psychiatrist, but short of growing up again in a different way I saw no hope of becoming a different person. Like it or not, I was the sum of my yesterdays and there was no way I could change my personal history. Instead of producing happiness my increased self-knowledge led to a dry resignation of my lot, and my reaction to life became a shrug of the shoulder. I became pessimistic about all people, seeing them as flawed, wrong somehow, with no way to be made right. It seemed clear that no amount of culture or affluence was going to change them—or me.

About this time my father became desperately ill and seemed at the point of death. The threatened loss of a major support in my life cracked what remained of my nice veneer. As the mask fell away, I was left exposed to those around me, a frightened child who didn't know who she was or what she was going to do with the rest of her life. My father recovered but following this emotional crisis I just didn't save the strength to pretend anymore. Of course the image of the perfect wife was shattered, but Bob, although he was bewildered, had far more genuine love for me than I had suspected. We began picking up the pieces— my husband, my psychiatrist, my doctor and I, all trying to put Nancy together again. They were wonderful and patient and gave me their concern even though I had nothing to offer in return, but it was rough going. Then, in the midst of this emotional turmoil I discovered that I was going to have another baby. This was the last straw! I couldn't manage the family I already had—what would I do with another child? What made my pregnancy almost unbearable was the possibility, acknowledged by my doctor, that for certain medical reasons the child might not be normal. He knew me well, and he recognized that my impulse would be "to run." He said, "Nancy, all your life you've run from anything unpleasant. I'll help you all I can to stand up and face whatever happens." Of course, I knew I couldn't face it, but at least I didn't have to think about it yet.

I have always loved to read, and as a child I had read and dreamed and pretended. Now, once again I found the same comfort in books. Every week I came home from the library loaded with a stack of books, wildly assorted ones—cookbooks, biographies, murder mysteries, and occasionally, something on religion. I enjoyed C. S. Lewis, but I wasn't sure I understood his explanation of Christianity. About this time my sister-in-law brought me a copy of the New Testament translated by J. B. Phillips. At first I was not inclined to bother with it because I had taken a Bible course in college and I had read the Bible for religion class as I had read *Moby Dick* for philosophy. My opinion then had been that both books were too long. Nevertheless, I began reading in the New Testament as I would have read a novel.

Much to my surprise the words were fresh and understandable in this modern translation. What I began as a diversion soon became arresting reading and then, disturbing. The Gospel of John was especially disturbing to me as the figure of Jesus began to come alive in those pages. He was compelling, magnetic, impossible to dismiss but not very believable in human terms. He seemed to have overwhelming things to say about the very questions I had been asking in my own life, yet somehow I couldn't *understand* what He was saying. What did He mean when He talked of losing your life to save it? The character that began to emerge was certainly not the Jesus meek and mild of Sunday school days. There was an uncompromising quality about Him that had authority. I had known for a long time that acceptance of the Church's teachings about Jesus as the Son of God was not enough for me anymore, but I did not know what else to do. Now, however, one fact became clear—I did *not* know who Jesus was.

The question of who Jesus was suddenly seemed very important to me. Was He a rabble-rousing Jewish carpenter with dreams of glory? Was He a lunatic who believed Himself to be God? Was He a good man unjustly executed for upsetting the order of things? Or could I accept His own claims for Himself, that He was in some strange way human and divine? Somehow, my interest in the subject seemed unexplainable, for I was increasingly irritated by anything religious. Even though I had continued going to church, I no longer felt the peace and serenity I had once sensed there. And going to church on Sunday certainly made no difference in the way I lived my life on Monday or even Sunday afternoon.

In spite of love, in spite of psychiatric help, in spite of all my own efforts to change, I came to a night which must be described as a night of ultimate despair. It was shortly before my twenty-ninth birthday, a time of reckoning, I suppose; and I knew that I could no longer fool myself. I was tired, and I thought, "I have done what I can and it isn't enough. If that psychiatrist reworks me another twenty years I'll still be wrong! What *is* it that's the matter with me?" Feeling that I had come to the end of things, I cried out, "Oh, God, if there is a God, You've got to help me, because I can't go another step by myself!"

In that moment I knew with a certainty that there was a God, that He cared about me, that I was not isolated in a cold universe, and that somehow I was going to be all right. It was not a vision, or a blinding light, or a thundering voice, but the sure knowledge of God's presence that could not be denied.

That night split my life into two parts.

. . . Jesus stood up and proclaimed, "If any one thirst, let him come to me and drink. He who believes in me, as the scripture has said, "Out of his heart shall flow rivers of living water."

John 7:37, 38 (RSV)

CHAPTER 3

CHAPTER 3

WATER AND THE WORD

In the days that followed I simply could not deny my experience of the reality of God, for I knew it had happened. Still, I wasn't sure what it meant, was afraid to tell anyone. I had never heard anyone mention an encounter with God, and I was certain my friends would think I was crazy if I did. In fact, the very word "God" was embarrassing to most of the people I knew outside the context of a religious situation. Perhaps my habit of hiding from people was part of my reluctance to talk to anyone about my experience, or perhaps I was afraid of the fragility of it—that it could disappear in the face of a blank stare. Whatever the reason for my silence, I simply treasured what had happened that night as a secret and precious thing, without explanation.

I turned back to the Bible, for this was the book that was all about God, and I needed to know more about Him and about the claims of Jesus of Nazareth. As I read the Gospel of John once more, I became excited. In the third chapter there was a curious story about a Jew named Nicodemus who came to see the man who was working miracles. Nicodemus started the conversation with Jesus by saying that he knew He was a teacher come from God or else He couldn't do those wondrous things. Jesus replied that no one could possibly understand the works of God unless he was *born again*. His answer puzzled me as much as it did Nicodemus, but I began to wonder if there could not be two birth experiences, one physical and the other spiritual. Was the *born again* incident an explanation of what had happened the night God became real to me? Reading on in the book of John, the whole story of the life and death of Jesus seemed incredible to me and I could not honestly admit that I understood it. It was hard to believe that Jesus rose from the dead, but His disciples were sure of it. If He did rise to life, was He alive today and did this mean something to me?

I worried and wondered and again read through C. S. Lewis' *Mere Christianity*. Though I could not be sure; though there were many questions for which I did not have the answers; though I could not put it all together; the suspicion grew within me that this story of the life and death and life again of the man called Jesus just might be bedrock truth. Perhaps in Jesus the Christ might be found the source of all life, the Absolute that I could never find before. He claimed this for Himself. "I myself am the road," replied Jesus, "and the truth and the life. No one approaches the Father except through me" (John 14:6).[1] As these words rolled through my mind, my certainty about Jesus grew. Leaping over what remained of my skepticism, I accepted Jesus at His word, as God in human flesh, the Savior who could somehow save me from myself.

In accepting Christ Jesus as who He said He was; in being willing to let Him do for me what He came to earth to do for all men—in this aceptance came the answer to the question I had asked about who I really was. "He came into his own crea-

---

[1] J. B. Phillips, *The New Testament in Modern English* (New York: The Macmillan Company, 1958), p. 221.

tion, and his own people would not accept him. Yet wherever men did accept him he gave them the power to become sons of God. These were the men who truly believed in him, and their birth depended not on the course of nature nor on any impulse or plan of man, but on God" (John 1:11-13).[2] I was a child of God and this was His world. I belonged. I had a place.

In reading more of the New Testament account of God's expression of love in Jesus Christ, I began to see that God must be the Author and Source of all love, even the love between human beings which is but a reflection of God's love. It was the sense of being loved that I had looked for all my life, in different ways, from different people. Knowing that I was now God's own child, I began to understand that in my relationship with Him I had all the love that I could ever need. It began to dawn on me that perhaps love does not exist except in a relationship, and love to be love must have an object. God, the full circle of love, evidently needs to have a responsive object for His love, a human being who is willing to be His, to belong to Him, to be committed to the God-man relationship. It was an awesome thing for me to realize that Almighty God wants, even needs, my response freely given; but in this idea I found the explanation for the mystery of creation. The creation of a man free to love or not love God was the risk He took to have the companionship of man, deliberately given to God. I could understand this by looking at my own relationship with my children—I would far rather have them love me for myself than just obey me because of my authority over them.

God gave me freedom of choice, and for most of my life I chose to be my own god. In making the important decisions of my life it had never occurred to me that God might enter into my choice, that He might have a purpose for my life. In pursuing my own goals I had learned the inevitable lesson, though; if you are going to play God, you need to be all-wise and all-powerful. I was neither.

---

[2] *Ibid.*, p. 186.

I now began to understand why Jesus had to come to earth. The turning away of man from God made necessary the coming of a new Man. God in His love and mercy provided a way out for self-centered mankind. In Jesus Christ, both God and man, is found the perfect relationship of love between the human creature and the divine Creator—He is the bridge between perfect God and imperfect me. That God loves me, this I am sure of, because He has shown me His love in so many ways. He has given me the very air I breathe. That I really love Him is another matter, for in all honesty I want my own way, not God's purpose for my life. But the new life of Christ implanted in my old nature can change the orientation of my life; Christ Jesus, perfect God and perfect man, gives me His risen life as a substitue for my own, that I may know the Father and love Him.

The knowledge of God's love for me, eternal and inexhaustible, began to free me from the desperate need to be loved by other human beings. All of my life I had fed my hunger with the perishable, imperfect love of those around me, and because most of my efforts were centered on *getting* love I had very little time to *give* love. It was now clear that I was a person of value because God found me worthy to the point of the sacrificial offering of His own Son. I could not penetrate the mystery of the Cross, but in some way Christ died for my wrongness; He died that I might be made right again. I didn't earn it; I don't deserve it; I can't buy what He gives to me. The best part of salvation was that I could relax in the warmth of His acceptance.

Once this became clear to me, not so much because I figured it all out, but because God's word said so; once I knew the truth and it set me free, then I began to free those around me. For years I had burdened parents, husband, children, friends with the necessity of loving me and making me happy. Because I was being freed from the pressure of winning love and approval, I began to offer my love to other people without the assurance in advance that it would be returned.

The basic relationships with those closest to me began to

change—not because I tried to change them, but because I was becoming a different person. I was still shy and reluctant to become involved with others in a way that might hurt me, but I saw in Christ's love the ultimate giving with no thought of return. Love became a sacrificial offering, the thing most acceptable in the sight of God. But learning to love is not easy, and I did not change overnight. I was not first one person and then another; rather, God began with me where I was and His process of re-creation is still continuing.

At this particular point in my life two things, two ideas were the areas on which God focused my attention. The first of these was love and the second was salvation. The word salvation had been for me a "glory" word, high-sounding but empty of meaning. It was a word used often and loosely by preachers and evangelists, but I had never really understood what they meant. In my new life, however, salvation became a word that had richness of meaning. It was a live option because it was happening to me.

Being saved is not something that takes place in the abstract. The aspects of it become very practical when you experience it. I don't attempt to define salvation in a theological way; it would be hard to improve on what the Scripture has to say in defining it. What I can do is show within the framework of my own life what salvation can mean. In probing my understanding of the word, three questions seemed inevitable. What was I saved from? And by whom? And for what purpose? I knew at the outset that I could not answer any of the three completely, but in the asking of them I have found new answers for myself about the puzzle of human existence.

From my Bible reading I began to understand that God has always had a plan. Actually this is obvious, even if the Bible didn't say so, because the world is orderly. It should be no harder to accept the spiritual order of things in the world than it is to accept the material order. The God who created both most surely knows what He is about, but most of us have difficulty with things we cannot see and touch. On the surface it is slightly absurd to claim reality for Jesus Christ. How can He be as real to me as my children are, for instance? My children are physical beings—I can see them and touch them. But all children have bodies, and what I know and love about my own youngsters is that mysterious uniqueness called personality. It isn't so strange, then, to claim reality for the greatest Personality in the universe —the Creator God born a man and resurrected to glory, the Christ Deity made flesh, risen above flesh, imperishable, all-powerful, eternal. To claim to know this Personality is awesome, even presumptuous, but it is the testimony of believers throughout the ages. I know Christ Jesus and this fact alters my life. It is as simple and as complex as that.

In looking back on the twenty-eight years of my life that were lived without the relationship to God in Christ Jesus I can see the results of my own efforts. God could do little for me until I admitted to myself and to Him my helplessness to effectively order my own life. God began to deal with me as I allowed Him to do so. Allowing God to come into my everyday situation meant that I offered Him a tentative surrender of my will into His keeping. I understood my will to be my sovereignty, my right to make my own decisions. I made what Sam Shoemaker calls "an experiment of faith." I committed an area of my life that was defeated to see what God could do with it.

My desire to escape the unpleasantness of life expressed itself in drinking Martinis or taking tranquillizers, and up to this point my resolutions and wrestlings with this very real problem had come to just about nothing. I'd get in a tight spot emotionally and want to run. I surrendered to God my own helplessness to change my reaction to tense situations. What began to emerge as God's response to my need was not a dramatic refusal of alcohol or pills, but a soft, insistent check at the critical moment of choice. I learned that God's strength could carry the day for me in my emotional turmoil. I now had something stronger, of more value to me than the sense-dulling peace of a tranquilizer or a drink.

The world of difference was in God's power at work in my life; I did not just make new resolutions. Resolutions I had made a hundred times; and what I had promised, even at God's altar, I could not keep in my own strength. This experience of learning that God in Christ could be the power as well as the motivation changed every area of my life. What Paul said in the book of Philippians became real in my own situation: "I can do all things in him who strengthens me." (Philippians 4:13 RSV) It became possible to face that fact that my child, soon to be born, might in some way be less than a normal baby. I was still frightened, but underneath the fear was assurance that God could give me courage for even this.

On Palm Sunday, 1963, our little daughter was born, a perfectly normal, beautiful child; but she was tiny because she was very premature. It was a sunshiny Sunday morning until our pediatrician came in and said, "I want to be honest with you. I don't think your little girl is going to live. Her lungs are immature and she's having trouble breathing." I said to myself, "Dear God, You just can't do this to me, not after all I've been through! This baby girl is mine and I want her." As I said the word "mine" I knew that she really wasn't mine. She belonged to God, even as I belonged to Him, and in that moment I opened my hand on the child, committing her to God's care and His perfect will. Throughout the day I was calm. Bob called in all the doctors he knew, but we both were aware that little could be done for her except to keep her in an oxygen-filled incubator. At the end of the day the doctor came back into my room and told us that she was improving steadily and he felt she would live. There was never a more grateful heart than mine that night, and our little girl, Jennifer, is a living reminder to me of God's love.

Who can spread his hours before him, saying,
"This is for God and this is for myself; This
is for my soul and this other for my body?"
The Prophet by Kahlil Gabran

CHAPTER 4

A NEW ALLEGIANCE

The first eight months of my new life were spent in solitary amazement at what God was doing, practically speaking, to change the kind of person I was. I learned to pray, to offer up to God the everyday events of my life and to give Him a chance to answer those prayers. Reading the Bible took on a new meaning even though there was much that I didn't understand. Attending church now meant a chance to worship my God, to show a special reverence for who Christ was. What had been frustration now became joy. I read many books on the Christian faith, and I particularly felt at home with C. S. Lewis, who was now my friend in Christ. I struggled through St. Augustine's *Confessions* and was delighted by his joyous hymn of praise to God. All of these things nourished me and I became ever more sure of the validity of my own faith, but I had no contact in a personal way with any other believer.

I did not know who to talk with about my new-found relationship with Jesus Christ. I could not bring myself to tell Bob about the drama of the new life that was unfolding in me. When we were first married I had pushed him into the Episcopal Church, and once he had been confirmed and had done what I wanted him to do, he dismissed the whole idea of religion. It was something he didn't need and he didn't want to waste Sunday morning going to church. In fact, my nagging about church attendance in years gone by had gradually built up a wall between us on the subject of religion. If I wanted to go to church it was fine with him; and if reading the Bible helped me with my emotional difficulties, then he didn't object, but he obviously thought Bible reading a little odd. While I was unable to talk to him about God and Jesus Christ, I did pray very earnestly that God would, in time, become real for him, too. I was even shy about going to my minister because I didn't know the right words to explain what was happening to me; in fact, my habit of reticence was still so strong that I could not yet talk to anyone about all that I knew God was doing.

In the summer of 1963 Bob and I were invited to a conference at a place called Laity Lodge, a layman's retreat center in the hill country of Texas. We didn't know very much about it except that a Baptist layman from Corpus Christi named Howard Butt, Jr. was to be one of the speakers that weekend. I had never met Howard although we had lived in the same town for a number of years, but his wife, Barbara Dan, belonged to one of the organizations that I did, and I knew her slightly. The Butt family had built the center, which was supposed to be a very beautiful place. I had also heard that a man named Keith Miller was the Director of Laity Lodge, and that he was an Episcopalian. Except for this meager bit of information we knew nothing about it, but I had the strong feeling that this was the time for Bob and me to go to something like this together. Bob, of course, did not want to go. But this was one of the few times in our marriage that I insisted on having my own way, and he finally said he would take me. He resigned himself, but he didn't like it. At a party I overheard him tell a friend that next week he had to go to some religious place in the woods where everyone sat around in a circle and sang hymns. I didn't like bucking Bob's disapproval, but I prayed very hard for the courage to insist, and we went.

The Lodge was indeed a beautiful sight as we drove up to it. The main building was hung on a rock cliff overlooking the Frio River and across the river there was a wall of rock, soaring up to a stand of cedar trees on the ridge. The scenery and the buildings blended into a dramatic setting, all the more magnificent for its air of naturalness. We had arrived in time for the first evening meeting, a get-acquainted session. There were about fifty of us gathered in the large hall, and Keith Miller, after explaining a little about Laity Lodge, asked each of us in turn to introduce ourselves and say why we had come. Bob was the second person as we began to go around the circle, so he stood up and said, "My name is Bob Peerman, and I was dragged here! I don't buy any of this religious business because two and two is four and none of the answers in religion adds up right." Then he sat down and it was my turn to speak; at that moment I would have given anything to be someplace else!

But at that evening meeting the speaker was a man named Fred Smith, a management consultant for many large companies, who talked about how Christianity and business were in some ways similar. Bob listened intently, and when we got back to our room he began scribbling furiously on a scrap of paper. I asked Bob what he was doing and he replied, "Honey, this man has given me some great ideas on how to run my business!"

The next morning we listened to a pediatrician from Hopkinsville, Kentucky, who told a humorous story about how a young groceryman named Howard Butt had come to town and held some meetings, and that somehow his life had changed since that time. Bob turned to me and whispered, "I've just got to hear this Howard Butt, this thunder and lightning!"

The conference moved at a fast pace. After the morning session the large group was divided into four small groups for informal discussion. Our subject had to do with the Parable from

the Gospel of Luke about the Prodigal Son. The Prodigal was
the younger of two sons and he asked his father for his inheri-
tance so that he could go off to the far country to enjoy himself.
Predictably, he was soon penniless and so came home again. His
father welcomed him with joy, but the older brother felt angry
that his own loyalty to duty was not more appreciated by his
father. We were asked by our group leader to think about which
character in the story each of us identified with. I felt in a sense
that I was both the older brother and younger—I had stayed in
church all these years, but at the same time I had been separated
from my real spiritual home. Bob's reaction to the parable was
that he was the younger brother, still in the far country, only he
hadn't run out of money yet.

There was free time after lunch, time to swim or wander
around or just to think. I am sure that there was a lot of thinking
going on that afternoon. I had resolved that I would not try to
talk to Bob, that somehow he was in God's hands, not mine. The
outcome of the weekend for him was beyond my control. Besides, there were pressures coming to bear on my own understanding.

That evening Bob got his wish; Howard Butt was the speaker.
As Howard began, Bob folded his arms as if to say, "You just
show me that thunder and lightning." And thirty minutes later,
from the dumb-founded look on Bob's face, I knew that lightning had struck. Howard had simply presented the claims that
Christ had made for Himself—that He was King, that He was
the Son of God, that He had come into the world to save it, that
He was in some mysterious way God . . . and man. As Howard
talked on, he had explained that a man could somehow be related to God through Jesus Christ.

Bob didn't say much to me then, but I knew that something
was happening, and I gave thanks to God, because a miracle was
taking place before my eyes. Later Bob told me of some of his
feelings that weekend. He said, "I guess I had sort of been my
own god for a long time. I had told myself I could handle my

own life, but deep down I was really afraid that if something awful happened, like going bankrupt, I wouldn't be able to take it. Underneath my big front I was just a little boy. And when Howard talked about being related to God, something way down inside me wanted that relationship. I wanted to belong to God. So I decided to try out this relationship, to see if it would really work. And, you know, it really did."

That weekend was the beginning of Bob's commitment to God in his new understanding of who Jesus Christ was. I was amazed and overjoyed by what was taking place in his life, but beyond that, our time at Laity Lodge was special for me, too, in a different way. It was a homecoming for me, for I had found *my* people. Among those there for the weekend were people who knew Jesus the way I had come to know Him and they were living the same life of faith that I was; but they were able to speak openly about their relationship to God in Christ Jesus and to share with all of us some of their own personal experiences. For the first time I heard a Christian witness, a woman who was a member of my own church in Corpus Christi. As she told of the meaning of Christ in her life, I was amazed, for I had known her casually for a long time. But now I thought, "She and I are sisters. I'm not so different after all; this is real and I'm part of what these people are talking about." Although I was too shy to say much to anyone, this was the beginning for me of reaching out to other people to share something of my own life in Christ.

More important than homecoming, though, was the challenge that Keith Miller offered to me in one of his talks. He suggested that Christ wanted to be not only the Savior but the Lord of my life. There was no doubt in my heart that He was my Savior; He had saved me from myself and the consequences of my own mistakes. What Keith was talking about was the surrender of self, commitment of the will on a deeper level than I had thought about before. Out of love and gratitude I wanted to do something for Christ, but I could not truthfully say that I wanted to give up myself, my right to make decisions to anyone, even God.

I could offer this much—"Lord, I want to want You that much. Please take me at this point and help me to want You more than anything else in the world." And I believe that He *did* take me at this point, for at least I acknowledged that my life was not my own; I knew to whom I belonged. And the Lord Jesus Christ continues to work out His Lordship over my life.

What I gave up, however, when I "gave up myself" to Christ Jesus was my own limited view of myself—my faults, my virtues, all the preconceived notions that I have about a person called "me." I lost this view in order to be free to see myself in God's eyes, perfected by the life and completeness of His own Son. This is the *losing of life* in order to find it. Actually, I traded a very poor sort of life for the fullest life of Christ.

One result of that weekend was the formation of a Bible study group in Corpus Christi. Most of the people who participated in the conference wanted to learn more about the Bible and what the Christian life was like. We began meeting every Tuesday night with Howard Butt as our leader and teacher. There were about sixty of us, and among our number were some unlikely candidates for Bible study. Most of us knew little about the Bible or about Christianity, but at Laity Lodge we had caught a glimpse of a vitality, a freshness of life that attracted us. Bob was reasonably typical of our group, although perhaps a bit more honest than some of us. We had been meeting for several sessions when he finally spoke up and said, "Could someone tell me who this Paul was?"

The first hour of the meeting was spent in listening to Howard's enlargement of the principles of Christianity that we were studying in John Stott's book, *Basic Christianity*. After that we broke up into four small groups for a discussion of the portion of Scriptures we were reading. We agreed to pray for the other members of our small group every day by name. In the intimacy of this smaller gathering those of us new to the Christian life were introduced not only to God's Word, but to the love offered to us by those who were our spiritual guides. For the next two years we met together regularly, and in that time we learned to read the Bible daily, to pray, and to share our experiences and difficulties. Bob and I looked forward to Tuesday night, because at the meeting there was an excitement and joy that we didn't find other places.

The small group approach to Christian growth and development is one of the most dynamic tools available to the Christian Church today. The idea is far from new, for the early Church met in homes, and in each generation since that time believers have gathered in twos and threes. But particularly in these days of large church congregations and impersonal communities is the small study and prayer group necessary; however it does not by any means take the place of the Church itself. The Church is because Christ is; it does not exist for itself but to serve its Head. The Church is the fellowship of all believers here on earth, and it was brought into being by God Himself. It has been many things throughout the ages—a small Jewish sect, meeting in secret; custodian of the Faith in troubled times; a power to be reckoned with during the political struggles of the Middle Ages; a respectable society of the "best" people. It has been many things, sacred and profane, and it suffers because its members are human and make mistakes. The Christian Church of today is the same; it is right and wrong, good and bad, real and false, but it is the Church of God and its present members are linked back through all the generations to Christ Himself. It is more than an institution. It lives and breathes and moves as its people do, but it owes its life to God. It exists not to build monuments or guard morals or safeguard the Faith; it may need to do these things, but it exists to serve the Lord Jesus.

In a sense the Church is able to serve Christ in a collective way only as it is made up of obedient individuals who are willing to perform their unique function. In the twelfth chapter of 1 Corinthians Paul speaks of the Church in terms of the human body and its various parts. A friend of mine had broken her big toe and her comment about the situation was that she had never realized how important that toe was to the way she lived her life. Each Christian has a special role to play in the life of the Body of Christ, the Church. The accomplishment of God's purpose in the everyday, all-around-us world, depends on the creative response of a person to His God; it is no good trying to substitute the institution for the individual.

I have seen many individual Christians grow in small groups and become useful servants of Christ in their own churches. Nevertheless, the response of the organized Church to the idea of Christians meeting together in homes is sometimes suspicious hostility. It is true that some groups are not well-grounded in the principles of the Christian faith, but reliance on the Scriptures themselves is a vital part of the effectiveness of the group. The concept of a small group of Christian laymen meeting in Christ's name is as old as the New Testament itself. Now, as then, these groups are a real help to many people.

God often speaks to me through the members of the group with whom I'm meeting. Quite often, it seems, I do not want to hear what He would say to me through other Christians because it hits too close to my pride. For example, during the time we were meeting with our first group I had to face the concept of the Scriptures in regard to the relationship of husband and wife. Paul is pretty pointed about who he thinks should be the head of the household (Ephesians 5:22), and, as an emancipated woman, I resented what this implied. Our group discussed this passage of Scripture and my friends would not leave me alone about my attitude until I had resolved my problem of pride. Fortunately, I have several close Christian friends who are tuned into my wave-length because they can usually put their finger on my sore spot—the thing I am protecting in a self-centered way. This constructive criticism can only operate effectively in the context of love and concern, for honesty and hostility can be a devastating combination.

Since that first experience, Bob and I have participated in many different groups. The members have varied widely in background, denomination, and understanding, but the "magic" is always there. The requirements for a group like this are simple—openness to God's Holy Spirit; willingness to be honest about oneself; a feeling of concern for the welfare of other members of the group; a commitment to do the work involved in study. This kind of group has special meaning to me because it was in one of them that I learned how to be a real person, to respond to others in a natural way. I had been ingrown for so long that my response was slow and painful, but I learned to be open and to dare to be myself. The Book of Common Prayer of the Episcopal Church contains a beautiful phrase, "the company of all faithful people." This seems descriptive of the great host of Christians who find together in the presence of God and each other a depth and richness of human relationship that could never be theirs except on the terms of the Holy Spirit.

When you love you should not say, "God is in my heart," but rather, "I am in the heart of God."

The Prophet by Kahlil Gibran

CHAPTER 5

CHAPTER 5

THE SECOND GREAT COMMANDMENT

In my experience, neutral ground was safe ground and I have usually chosen to do the conventional, approved-of thing. I wanted to avoid the disapproval of others and to do so I was careful not to commit myself to anything to an extreme degree. Although my father had raised me in a liberal political tradition, I quickly learned in college that it was a conservative philosophy that dominated the upper-middle class world to which I belonged. My solution was to become non-political rather than choose a side, and this was typical in general of my reaction to the issues of life. At Laity Lodge I faced my reluctance to choose and realized that it isn't really possible to be neutral—like it or not each of us chooses what will have first place in our lives. At one point in my life I had put scholastic achievement first; then I wanted to be a success in the social world; later I wanted to be the perfect wife. For Bob, what came first was the success of his business and the power and pleasure that success brought him. These are commitments, priorities; and whatever they are, they play a tremendous part in the shaping of our lives. As I began to understand this, it became clear that the weak but honest commitment of my life to Jesus Christ would completely change its orientation.

Upon deciding to take seriously the claims of Christ on my life, things began to happen; I began to be involved as a real person with other persons. This was surprising because honest involvement with people was something I had always avoided. In a sense I shouldn't have been surprised because Jesus in His life on earth was continually involved with real people and their real difficulties. He wasn't the least bit particular about their social status or their moral condition. His life was full of people because people were important to Him.

In coming to know Christ as my Savior I had found the way to handle my own particular problems; and as my reactions changed, the emotional climate of my life changed. Now it began to be tidier than before, and happier, too. But in coming to an awareness of Christ as Lord and responding to it with the surrender of my right to myself I began to move out of my own comfortable life into the wider world of other people's needs.

The first and most practical instance of this came in relation to my own home and my role as wife and mother. I have never been much of a housekeeper. It always seemed so dull and uninteresting, especially when it just had to be redone the next day, but God began to show me that if this was my job in life then I ought to be a little better at it. At the same time I became more aware of my husband and children as people to whom I could really mean something. It is so easy for human beings to live in the same house and yet be uninvolved with each other—husband and wife, parents and children, living out life as strangers. In obtaining insight into my own situation I saw that as a wife and mother, I had the unique opportunity to create an atmosphere of warmth and concern in which those around me could flourish. But this could happen only as I put God first in my life and stopped insisting that things be arranged especially to suit me.

Seeing myself as God's own child, created different from all His other children, I had to accept my husband and children in the same light. It was a shock to both Bob and me to realize that our children did not literally belong to us—that they were ours to nurture and love, but we didn't own them. They must be free to be themselves, not what we felt they ought to be. This did not mean extreme permissiveness; in fact, I became firmer with them than I had been before, for I recognized in a new way my responsibility before God for their care and nurture.

Then too, I came to understand the necessity of communication with the children at *their* point of interest, not mine. For example, I had been disappointed that my two boys did not share my love of reading. While they had no reading difficulties in school, they just didn't spend much time reading at home. I had been guiding their selection of books, but finally it occurred to me that I needed to let them read what *they* found interesting. Since then they have literally devoured dozens of "Hardy Boys" and sports books, and while they haven't read any of the great children's classics yet, they may in time. And in playing with our baby daughter I had to learn to play *her* games in a whole-hearted way; even a small child senses a lack of interest. Knowing that my interests are primarily in "adult things," I asked for God's help in this special way, and my new understanding of children as God's children even made it easier to put my heart into reading "The Three Bears."

As a wife, I had felt that married couples ought to do things together whether they enjoyed them or not. I dragged Bob to operas that bored him, and he bought a small airplane for us to travel in, though I hate to fly. The idea of togetherness is sometimes grim, and however compatible two persons' interests are, there are always areas of difference. Bob and I share many interests, but our points of view about the same thing are apt to be quite different. In coming to respect and accept my own personality as unique, created by God, I also came to respect and accept my husband's right to do certain things. If he wanted to watch two football games on two separate television sets at the same time, it was all right with me. What I used to resent because I wasn't included can now be accepted as part of the wonderful difference between Bob and me. I believe this applies to the deepest level of marriage, to the basic difference between man and woman. So many marriages break down at this point because each partner tries to change the other. I am a modern woman, raised to believe that men are no better than women, and I still think this is true. But man is different from woman and each is happiest in accepting that difference.

With my mother and father I found that I was growing into a new relationship based on a more realistic view of their roles in my life as an adult. I am sure that the inter-play of personalities between grown children and parents is one of the most sensitive because it involves a shift of dependence and a realignment of responsibility. I had to learn to know them in a different way, and once I was freed from emotions left over from childhood I was able to seek a warmer relationship with my parents. One of the lessons that was hard for me to learn was to refrain from trying to tell *them* what to do; I am sure that many well-meaning children offend their parents by assuming that now they know what's best for the people who have raised them. I am grateful that I have had the opportunity to be friends with them, and my father and mother have come to mean more to me than ever before.

It would have been easy for me to stop at the limits of my own satisfying world, for at last I was contented in being who I was, and I found joy in my husband, my home, my children, my parents. Bob was growing tremendously in his life with Christ, and sharing our insights gave a new dimension to our marriage. Both of us had talked a little to friends, trying to describe what had taken place in our lives, but we did not find it easy to come right out and talk about Jesus Christ. Our commitment to Him seemed very personal to us, and we were aware of how silly it all might sound to our old swinging crowd.

After our Bible study group had met for about four months, Howard Butt asked Bob to speak informally to our group, to witness to his new life in Christ. He agreed because he thought a lot of Howard, but he was so nervous beforehand that I wasn't sure he'd go to the meeting. But when he stood up before the group and began to tell his story, it was all right. He was honest, he was funny, and in his own way he told of the power of God in his life. Several weeks later Keith Miller invited us back to the Lodge for another weekend conference, this time to witness as part of the program. If Bob was nervous, I was petrified, and I could not believe that I could stand up in front of people to tell them about myself and the reality of Christ in an honest way. I was still a little afraid of people and the thought of rejection was painful. The story that I told was in outline what I have written about here, and once I had begun, God gave me a calmness and assurance that carried me through. Both Bob and I felt that we had done our part in witnessing and that this would probably be the last time we would be asked to do so; but three years later we are still being asked to witness to God's power and glory and so we are still doing it. We have been involved with many wonderful people in many different places these past three years. And although we are usually thanked "for coming," the blessing in doing this has always been ours. In going to various retreats and conferences we have come to know people in a new way, for the sharing of Christ is a strong basis for friendship.

It would be less than honest not to admit that there is a negative side as far as relationships with others is concerned. I must deal every day with my feelings, and at times what I feel is not love but resentment. And these resentments must be worked out —for my own sake as well as for those whom I resent. I can neither love nor hate without being affected myself in some way, and dealing effectively with resentments is a step toward emotional well-being. The Lord's Prayer speaks of the necessity of our forgiveness of others, but how can you forgive when you still resent? It is not enough to say, "I forgive her for the mean thing she said to me." If my feelings are hurt, I cannot simply pretend that they are not.

I have struggled to rid myself of stubborn grudges and unkind thoughts about people who have wounded me, and in trying to deal with this unlovely side of my nature I have arrived at a concrete way of surrendering my feelings of hate to God. I have to call it hate because that's what it is—resentment is a nicer word, but hate is more accurate. During much of my life I have denied strong feelings, especially strong negative feelings, and that denial has done nothing except increase my anxiety and guilt. In trying to shove out of consciousness all that is not loving I create a festering wound, uncleansed and uncauterized.

It helps me to write down my complaints, my charges against the accused. "She is not being considerate of my feelings. She is self-centered and just wants her own way. She shouldn't think she knows more than I do." In writing down these charges several things happen to me. First, I remove my resentments from the vague realm of just being mad. Moving from the general to the particular, I am freed from the squirrel cage of anger. Second, I gain insight into the fact that my own point of view is generally self-centered. What I usually resent most is that someone else does not see a situation from my viewpoint and therefore does not agree with me. As I see the limitations of my own perspective, I can look at the motives of the other person in a fresh way. I begin to see how *his* point of view influences his understanding of me, and as I understand him, I can forgive. I acknowledge my own limitations and I forgive him his. The healing of the wound begins to take place and God's grace can once again operate in my life.

People come in a package. In a sense I would like to split them up into what is acceptable and what is unacceptable, *according to my standards*. I tend to expect perfection from others, even though I know that it is impossible standard for any human being. Christians sometimes judge each other harshly, and it is true that the standards for a Christian are high. Inconsistencies in the lives of Christians are often an excuse used by non-Christians for not accepting the Faith. It is absolutely true that we who bear Christ's name are not worthy, but the point has never been worthiness or perfection of conduct, but faith in the worthiness and perfection of Jesus Christ, who imparts to His followers something of His own righteousness.

Needless to say, I destroy every such list, for seldom do I want anyone to know of my resentments. As I write them down I usually see how petty they are. God has dealt with them in my life, so He will deal with them in the other person's life. Occasionally I do feel that I must confront someone about something, but in doing so it is essential that my own attitude and motive be examined first. Honesty is a wonderful thing, but it should not be used as a knife. I have a little slogan—don't tell all you know to everyone all the time. To spew resentments onto those around you usually makes things worse. We know a couple who had kept score on hurts and resentments for twenty years, and each of them had total recall about the other's mistakes. They both met God in a new way at a laymen's meeting, and they were able to offer up to God all their hurts. Each of them laid down their sword and shield and began a new life together. They faced their resentments and got rid of them. The poison of unforgiven, unforgotten wrongs had almost killed their marriage.

Undoubtedly, if I were not so concerned about myself, I would be free of much of my vulnerability to resentment. I believe that for a Christian, whose life should be centered in Jesus and not himself, it is a sin to be offended. My level of self-centeredness may be gauged by how many of the people around me seem to be stepping on my toes. If I feel that the world just isn't treating me right, then I may be very certain that once again I have placed my own interests in the center of the stage. I can see in my children some of the ways self-centeredness operates. My three year old daughter is winsome, loving, and charming, but she certainly has a mind of her own. She cannot understand why she can't have a popsicle for breakfast, because that is what she *wants*. The human infant makes immediate demands on his environment—he must receive comforts like food and warmth and he screams for what he needs. During childhood most of us learn to yield to the needs and wishes of others so that we can all get along together in this world. But I am still that baby at heart. That is why I need Jesus Christ and His new nature.

Commitment of your life to Christ is a most solemn thing and you have no promise in advance as to where that commitment may lead. Do not ask lightly to be involved in God's work, for His work is the reconciliation of a lost world to Himself. The price of this reconciliation was the death of the Son of God; it may be costly for the Christian who offers himself to God for His use. It may not cost you your life, but it will cost you many other things—pride, money, time, comfort—and you may find that your self-sacrifice will not earn you the appreciation of the world. Indeed you may find a few rocks flying your way, but to be God's person in this world is most surely an exciting way to live.

. . . He leads me beside the still *and* restful
waters.

Psalms 23:2 (The Amplified Bible)

CHAPTER 6

THE GUIDING HAND

As Bob and I have participated in different conferences and groups, we have noticed that certain questions about the Christian life are almost certain to be asked. In discussion of the surrender of the right to oneself is the implied question of how God guides those persons who are willing to be guided. "How do I know God's will for my life?"—this is a very practical question because it deals with where we live, but it is a hard one to answer.

We found that the first step in finding guidance for our lives was for us to be clear about our relationship to God in the acceptance of Christ Jesus as the way into the presence of God. It is a comforting modern thought to believe that all men are God's children, and in the sense that He created all of us, we are indeed His creatures. But the Scriptures teach that all men are separated from God until they are bought back, made right again by Christ and His offering of Himself on the cross as payment for sin. It seemed foolish to expect God to guide us if we were separated from Him. I saw that I could not guide my own children if I had no real contact with them—separated, my influence would not be a force in their development.

Another problem to be faced in understanding guidance is the attitude one has toward the operation of God's will in an individual life. Do you really believe that Almighty God is interested in the everyday details of your life? For some very sincere Christians there is no such thing as moment by moment guidance by the Divine; they feel that God has given each of us a mind and a conscience and He expects us to use them. These are the do-it-yourself Christians who try to follow Christ's ethical example, and they are certainly to be commended for their efforts. But human wisdom isn't up to God's standards, at least mine isn't, and for me the outcome of this approach was a feeling of defeat. I tried, but I knew that I just wasn't measuring up, and I felt very guilty that I couldn't make my life work out smoothly. If it all depended on soundness of mind and character, then I was sunk. There had to be a source of strength and wisdom beyond my human limitations, for I had come to believe that God wanted wholeness and happiness for me, for each of His children. When Jesus talked about His purpose in coming, He spoke in terms of giving life and giving it in abundance.

One of the great affirmations of the Christian faith set forth in the Scriptures is that God is always faithful to His purpose. He is not available one day and out of touch the next. He does not change His mind, nor shift His purpose with the tide of human events. When the Gospel of John speaks of the Holy Spirit coming to guide us into all truth (John 16:13), I believe what it says —God has provided a means of guidance available all the time to those who are willing to be guided. It would be a strange thing for God to say that He wants our will—that He wants to use us as His servants in the world and then fail to provide the means of accomplishing that end. It is at this point that the Holy Spirit becomes real to me. I am grateful that I happened to read two very fine books on the subject of God's will and guidance: *The Christian's Secret of a Happy Life* by Hannah Whitall

Smith and *Beyond Ourselves* by Catherine Marshall. These books offer two very positive testimonies to the reality of the day-to-day guidance of God.

The practical-minded person still insists, "How do I know what God's will is;?" and the answer must seem evasive, for understanding God's will is a tentative thing, learned as you go along in the Christian life. I don't pretend to know in every instance what God would have me do, but in looking back over these past few years I believe that the changes in the way I have lived can only be the result of the guiding hand of God. One thing I am certain of is that to ask for God's will is to ask to be obedient, for guidance and obedience cannot be separated. At breakfast one morning Bob prayed, "Lord, we ask You to lead us this day," and as he said the words, the thought flashed into my mind that God can lead only if we follow. "To follow" is an active verb; it requires doing something, moving out. I believe that it was God's will that Bob and I go to Laity Lodge and that He directed me toward that goal; but I had to be willing to insist that we go. I have often asked for guidance and then sat back to see what happened. Sometimes God may be waiting for me to do that thing which He has already shown me. I am equally sure that the common sense approach is not always the direction God would have us go. Common sense is the collective wisdom of the race, and the common sense thing is usually that which is in my own best interest. I have to trust God and know that He Himself wills what is really best for me, for He does not always approach situations the way I would!

When I first became conscious of trying to do the thing God wanted me to do, I felt very tense about staying in touch. It was wearing to be constantly seeking guidance, but I was helped by another Christian who described his same difficulties in this way. He said, "I thought of God's guidance as operating like a radio, and I was forever tuning my radio to see if God was still transmitting and if I was still receiving. After much frustration I decided to assume that the radio was always operating and that

God could always get in touch with me if He wanted to." This little idea helped me to relax, knowing that God had promised to be with me always.

When I do feel unclear about direction in any situation—and most situations don't seem to be black or white—I ask myself a series of questions. For example two years ago I had to make a decision which would affect the use of my time, my role as wife and mother, and my view of myself as a productive person. From the time that Bob first went into the building business as a designer and contractor, I had helped him in various capacities as secretary, decorator, bookkeeper, ad-writer or any other role that was needed. I felt very useful, important to him because I saved him money, and when his office was at home it wasn't too hard to combine activities of homemaker and helpmate. As the years went by, he moved to larger offices and hired more help, but there were always things that no one else could do as well as I could (I thought) and between the business and our increasing involvement in Christian lay activities, I was away from home far too much. My two boys were school age, but our little girl was only a baby. I wrestled with the problem, but the three-way stretch kept pulling me apart. Something had to change, so I asked for God's help in deciding what to do.

What was the situation I was facing, honestly? It was a question of personal satisfaction and priority, and I had to decide what should come first—business, home, Christian service. It should have been easy to arrange them one, two, three, but I still wasn't alloting my time that way, so I had to ask myself another question. Why did I react to the situation the way that I did? In asking this I admitted to myself that I was afraid that being just a homemaker would not satisfy me, that I'd be bored if I gave up the stimulation of outside work. I was frightened, too, that I'd find out that I wasn't very essential to Bob's business and that he could get along so well without me that he wouldn't even talk over the business with me anymore. Then I wondered, can God really work in this situation? I knew how creatively He had worked in my life before, straightening out some of my mistakes, but I was tempted to feel that He might not know best in *this* situation. Finally I decided to trust Him once again, as I had trusted Him before. This led to the fourth question. Will I act on the knowledge that He is guiding me? As I felt more and more fragmented by my triple role, I knew that my choice was being made; and taking the plunge I retired from the business world. I had emotional adjustments to make and there were times that I felt restless, but in living out my choice I have come to know that it was the right one. These past two years I have had the freedom to do some of the things I've always planned to do, like writing; I have had time for people, to listen to them; and I have had the pleasure of watching a baby girl grow up into a little girl. Now I wonder why I hesitated, for it seems very simple, looking back; but the indecision at the time was very real and I needed God's help to break my inertia. Like a trapeze artist—I had to let go of one trapeze before I could take hold of another, and it was the moment in mid-air that was frightening.

God provides ways for each of us to learn what He would have us do, and I think perhaps these ways vary some for different people. A member of our group said that her strongest sense of guidance had come in God's checking hand. During a confused period of her life she had tried to put into operation her own solution to her problems, but try as hard as she would, she could not bring her plans to pass. It was only as she gave up and submitted to God's plans for her life that the situation began to work out, though it was a different solution than her own. This is guidance of the roadblock type, and I am sure that many of us have experienced something of this nature in our own lives.

I find guidance for my own life in prayer, Bible reading, and fellowship with other Christians, but there is also a solitary pursuit of God's will above and beyond these. I call it sensitivity to God's presence in my life. It is not easy to explain, for this is not a practical matter with definite conclusions to be reached. Spiritual awareness is a characteristic of personality and I can share what I have perceived, but perception is a very personal thing, differing with each human personality.

There is far more going on around us than we can see. In taking an art appreciation course I realized that I was not seeing much of what was passing before my eyes during an ordinary day. I was not conscious of many colors, shapes, and images that were all around me; but worse was the fact that in my self-centered way I tended to think that what I actually saw was all there was to see. For instance, when I finally swallowed my pride and got glasses for driving, I remember the shock of seeing details that I missed before. Being aware spiritually is much the same as being aware visually—there is far more going on in God's world, in people, in relationships, than I am able to comprehend. My comprehension limits my understanding of God's purpose and His way of fulfilling His purpose. It is not that it isn't happening; it's that I'm not aware that it is happening and I need a new pair of eyes.

As Christians we come to realize that the material world in which we live is not the real world, the world without end of which Christ spoke. We know that for each of us, as surely as death, this world is going to end. The Bible tells us that as Christians we are strangers in this *present* world, and that it is the *spiritual* world, so hard for us to understand, that endures forever.

Time, for instance, is a dimension of our present world, but it does not have the same meaning in terms of the spiritual world. In my present limited state eternity is a word that I don't understand. My three-year-old child asks, "Is this tomorrow?" and I can't find the words to explain to her. Even though I can remember yesterday and anticipate tomorrow, all I really have as far as time is concerned is this present moment. As I understand it, and I must give credit to C. S. Lewis for helping me, God lives in all moments at once, with no past, present, or future. I had been puzzled about how it is possible for God to give me free will, to allow me to make my own choices but know in advance what I am going to do. I can now see that the answer lies in the difference between time and eternity. God sees all my moments, as He also knows both the beginning and the end of the world. Where does a circle begin or end? The Bible speaks of God's plan, the beginning and the end, and yet Jesus offers eternal life to those who believe in Him. It is a paradox, and the strangest part of the paradox is that the two worlds coexist, material and spiritual, temporal and eternal, and the Christian lives in both at the same time.

My attitude toward death is bound up with this sense of the eternal order of things. I had to face my own feelings about death eighteen months ago when my father died. He had lived beyond the age of most men so his death was not a surprise. It was a shock, though—death is always a shock because it is so final. In the last days of his illness we had talked a good bit about God and I had found to my surprise that Christ had been real to him as the Son of God since he had accepted Him as a little boy. His father had been a Baptist minister, and he had rebelled in classic fashion against being the minister's son. His life had not been an overtly religious one, but during these last years he had been stirred by the telecasts of the Billy Graham Crusades. He died peacefully and unafraid; he died a Christian. This knowledge comforted me as I grappled with the hard fact that now I had no earthly father. The Episcopal Church has a glorious burial service beginning with the words, "I am the resurrection and the life." It is a spare, beautiful expression of the Christian hope, and the service itself ministered to me and to my mother. When it was all over, though, I had to face what I really believed. Was this man, my father, really gone, not gone anywhere, but just gone? In that moment of grief and doubt God graciously reminded me of His promises which are enough to live by and enough to die by. My father was with His Father.

In looking back I can see that even as a child I sensed that there had to be something larger than the life that I saw around me. This feeling expressed itself in an intense interest in mythology; I read Bulfinch's *Mythology* a dozen times. All the Greek and Roman gods and goddesses filled the need I had for something larger than human life. Perhaps in growing up I was aware of too much too soon, but at any rate I was never very optimistic about the here and now. I could somehow see to the end of possessions, relationships, desires, ambitions; life did not seem permanent to me. I wanted something without an end. In the mystery of Christ on the cross, the expression of God suffering for man; in His resurrection and His promise of everlasting life; in these I found my world without end. God is an inescapable fact for me now, and I cannot live without Him anymore.

To be honest, however, I know I would sometimes like to escape from the sureness of God's presence in my life. This knowledge imposes a price to pay in human terms, for knowing Him forces a choice between surrender of self and rebellion against His claims of Lordship. My initial surrender was made at Laity Lodge that first weekend, but surrender of the will is both a one-time and some-time thing. I surrender daily because I rebel daily. I can summarize my situation in this way. Suppose I am the owner of a field, rough and overgrown, like the kind found in the brush country of Texas. In a particular transaction I give title to the land to someone else. It is done and I don't own the field anymore. It will take the new owner, however, a long time to clear the land and make it productive. The anology is imperfect, but this is the way I understand surrender to Christ. I belong to Him, but I'm not much of a bargain yet.

The realization of my real position in this world helps me to become spiritually aware, but there is a danger in such awareness. For the person who by natural bent is sensitive to what is going on around him there is the possibility of being overcome by the depth and seriousness of life. Depression is a problem for a great many people, particularly those who have perception. The capacity to feel is a mixed blessing, for if a person experiences great joy, it should not surprise him that he also can experience great sadness. Sadness and joy are drunk from the same cup, and if I am really alive I cannot avoid living. Life is full of painful things

as well as joyous ones. In this sense Jesus shared our humanity—
the cup of crucifixion, the cup of resurrection, intermingled, bit-
ter and sweet. It is easy to accept the joy, but only God can give
the strength to embrace the sorrow. It is a paradox, but I have
found in that which was hardest to bear the understanding of
the measure of God's love for me.

Because I am introspective by nature I have found that it is
easy for me to drift into spiritual self-centeredness, a consciousness
of how everything around me is affecting me. Subjectivity and
spiritual perception are a tricky combination and without a firm
anchor in the objectivity of the life of Christ too much awareness
can sweep me away. I learn the same lesson again and again—
nothing I possess is good or right if I clutch it to myself. There
is only God's good and God's right. The absolute in the world is
faith in God through personal knowledge of Jesus Christ, the
One who is real to us because He became one of us. I must live
and experience the reality of God in order to know Him better;
and I have learned to look not for spiritual experiences, but for
the next step God has for me, however humdrum it may seem.
I've come to believe that we who call ourselves Christians are
not in the business of collecting answers; we are in the business
of walking in the light.

Men pass away, but the truth of the Lord endureth for ever. Without respect of persons God speaketh to us in divers manners.

The Imitation of Christ by Thomas Á Kempis

CHAPTER 7

CHAPTER 7

THE PAST AND PRESENT WORD OF GOD

Scripture and prayer, the past and present Word of God, seem to me to be two sides of the same coin. Neither would be of great importance if the life of the Christian began and ended with conversion, but rebirth is only the starting point of the purpose of God for my life. It is in the continuing revelation of God that I find understanding of myself and others. I know from experience that while it is faith that sustains, it is God's Word to me in prayer and in the Bible that gives my life breadth and depth.

Prayer was the first aspect of God's revelation that became real for me in my own situation. I turned to prayer in the earliest days of my born-again life as an answer to the puzzle of how to live my life in the way God wanted. Prayer was not new to me; Episcopalians spend a great deal of time on their knees in church, and I understood this form of corporate worship. It had always seemed reasonable to me to pray with those around me "for the whole state of Christ's church." What I had to begin to learn was that prayer could be conversation with God, and that it was

75

legitimate to pray not only for other people but for the ordinary things of my own life as well.

Abstract knowledge and actual experience are two very different things, and what I had to learn by doing was to talk with God and listen to what He had to say. This idea of dialogue with God seemed presumptuous to me until I realized that this was what my Father in Heaven wanted from me, His child. Once again my own children helped me see this. I cherish the times of give and take with my youngsters; there is a precious quality in these times of learning what each of them is like, at the moment. Private prayer, viewed in the same way, becomes not a duty but a delight, a time pleasing to God.

My first personal prayers were almost always cries for help. As I got into a tight spot emotionally, I would think, "God, You've got to help me, because I feel like I'm going to fall apart again!" I honestly admit that at critical times I didn't always ask for help, but when I did, He always gave it to me. I learned the value of spontaneous prayer, the momentary offering up of self at a red light, for instance. Instead of being annoying delays, red lights and stop signs became reminders in the midst of my busy world of carpools and errands of the eternal serenity of God. I began to pray for specific things for the people around me, and the amazing result was that I began to be interested in people I had never noticed before. The woman behind the counter at the cleaners became a real person to me, as I offered her up to God in the context of my dirty clothes. I began to pray for people I didn't like at all, and they became human, brothers not to be despised.

At the time I began seeking guidance in prayer I was involved in an unpleasant neighborhood situation. A neighbor had scolded my younger son, and although I had to admit that he deserved it, my motherly pride reacted badly to his tears. I didn't blow up, which is what I wanted to do, but by my coolness I let the neighbor know what I really thought. The whole mess was a thorn in my side, something I couldn't dismiss. At a Communion service at our church I offered this up as something that needed to be set right and I asked what I should do. Immediately I had the odd thought, "borrow their coffee pot!"

I had been getting ready to have a large group of people in my home and I needed a large coffee maker. But I was horrified with the idea of putting myself in the position of asking a favor of the couple I had snubbed. I thought, "Why, it would be easier to offer them a formal apology, except that I would have to admit how mad I had been. What if I ask them and they refuse?" It was impossible to dismiss what I felt that God wanted me to do, so I found myself on their front porch, ringing the doorbell. I'm sure they were surprised, but they were most gracious about the coffee pot. This was the beginning of a warmer relationship with my neighbors, but my conclusion from the incident is that I must be prepared for *anything*, if I submitted a matter in prayer to the will of God.

In spite of the simplicity of my early attempts at a prayer life as God's child, I have to admit that the farther I go in prayer, the more mysterious it seems. I can't understand it completely, or explain it in a satisfactory way, but I can't explain how electricity works either. I just know from my own experience what happens when I flip on the light switch. So it is with prayer, I know it works because I have seen it make a difference in my everyday life.

One of the most important prerequisites for finding out about the power of prayer is to approach prayer with an attitude of being open toward God. I often come to a time of prayer with a preconceived idea of what to pray for. I even suspect that I know exactly what God is going to say to me. These are the sterile times of prayer, for I have limited what I can receive from God. But any prayer time is refreshing to me, and in my life I need a regular time set aside for talking in an unhurried way with my God. I like to begin my day by acknowledging once again His Lordship. As the opportunity arises during the day, I take time for intercessory prayer and for a plain quiet time. I particularly need a few moments like this during the hour just before dinner, the "poison hour" when everyone is hungry and tired and cross. A break at that time is as refreshing to me as diving into a pool of water; the cares of the day fall away in the presence of Almighty God. There are days when I cut corners on prayer, but when I do my life gets a little ragged .

I have sometimes wondered how God answers prayers. I have come up with a funny little image about the way He might accomplish His purpose. If with an open heart I enter the great stream of God's will, I am in the company of other believers who do the same. I believe that God is able to communicate with all those who are His own. When I petition Him about something, He can use His other children in the fulfillment of my need. It is like a giant switchboard, with criss-crossing wires. I have often wondered how often God gets a busy signal from me.

After experiencing the joy of a private time with God, I began to be interested in the Scriptural idea of two or three persons joining together for the specific purpose of praying together. I had never been in a prayer group, and I didn't know how one could go about getting one together. I decided to pass the word around among friends that on the next Thursday afternoon at 1:00 there would be a meeting at my house to talk about forming a prayer group. I didn't issue specific invitations because I didn't want to pressure anyone, but that afternoon fifteen women came, including one I did not know at all. None of us knew what form the group should take, although I did have some suggestions from various books on the subject. We began by simply praying that the Holy Spirit show us what He wanted this group to be. This in itself required a good bit from all of us because none of us was very comfortable about praying out loud. I can remember the dry feeling in my mouth and the beating of my heart as'I tried to express to God in front of the other women what I hoped He would show us.

This group met every week, summer and winter, for eighteen months. In fact the group is still meeting, although I am now meeting with a new group, formed because there wasn't sufficient room to expand the first one as new women wanted to join. We developed a pattern for the meeting time itself—the first fifteen minutes is given to silence—what the Quakers call "settling in." After the period of quiet, we spend about an hour in discussion of the study material, and the last fifteen minutes we spend in praying together out loud. We accept the discipline of lifting each other up to God every day and of remembering the specific needs each of us has mentioned that week. There has developed a friendship and love between us all that is unbreakable, for we are all travelers together on the journey of faith. We share problems, blessings, defeats, and joys, and we have watched each other grow into a depth of faith that none of us had before. One of the most amazing things to me was that I, for the first time, felt comfortable with, and enjoyed the company of, other women. For so long, during my confused years, I had hated myself, and in a sense I had transferred that hate to all women. Now I would not miss the unique sharing that is mine with other women, and I hope that I will always have a group of friends with which to pray.

In thinking about my own life of prayer I have come to feel that there is a particular condition that we moderns need to bring to our time of prayer. A friend of mine speaks of prayer "in faith believing" and it is a phrase that I need to remember. It means in simple language that you approach prayer with the definite idea that God is not deaf, that He is faithful to those who ask His help, and that your prayer *will* be answered. Here I must have the help of God with my unbelief; it is so hard for my twentieth century mind to admit to miracles, even though I can see the miracle of my own new life in Christ. My first prayer, then, is always for simple faith, and my God answers even that prayer.

While prayer is a subjective means of knowing God and His will, the necessary balance to its subjectivity is found in the objectivity of the Bible, the record of God's dealings with the human race. Beginning with the Gospel of John, I gradually began to explore both the New Testament and the Old. For most of my life the Bible had been a book that was holy, dry, dusty, and a little old-fashioned. It was something to know about but not to read, and it had never seemed relevant to this modern age. Now I began to read it in a casual but serious way for what it could say to me about my own situation and for what I could learn about God.

The first thing that struck me was the amazing freshness of the Scriptures; its message was contemporary though it was written hundreds of years ago. When Jeremiah speaks of the human heart, he says that it is "deceitful above all things and desperately corrupt; who can understand it?" (Jeremiah 17:9 RSV) This is something I know about, right now. I know it in my own life; I read about it in the morning newspaper. This imperishable quality seems all the more unique when it is compared to scientific literature, for example. A medical book written fifty years ago is not the handbook I want my doctor to use in treating me today.

As I read more widely, I began to see the wholeness, the cohesiveness of the Bible—it says the same thing again and again. "We love because he first loved us." (1 John 4:19 RSV) "But God shows his love for us in that while we were yet sinners Christ died for us." (Romans 5:08 RSV) "He destined us in love to be his sons through Jesus Christ, according to the purpose of his will." (Ephesians 1:05 RSV) "For God so loved the world that he gave his only son, that whoever believes in him should not perish but have eternal life." (John 3:16 RSV)

Even as I quote these passages which have particular meaning for me—even as I set them down, I am reminded that it is the whole of Scripture, not what I select, that speaks what God would say. Heresies throughout the ages have come as the result of emphasis of one part of Scripture at the expense of the rest. There is meaning in it all, and if I let it, the Bible can be God's book for my life. The time I spend reading and studying the Word of God can make a real difference in what I do for the rest of the day. Yet I know that the Bible is not to be worshipped; faith in God through Christ Jesus is more important than any other thing. There have been many believers throughout the history of the Church who did not have direct access to the Scriptures. The current availability of the Bible tends to let us forget how recently printing was invented, and how in days past literacy was the privilege of the few. The earliest Christians had the Old Testament, but they did not have the New Testament at all— they were in the midst of writing it, of living out God's Word however it came to them. Perhaps there is narrowness today in our lives as Christians because we read and quote the Bible, but we don't live it out.

The Bible has practical advice for the everyday situations in which we find ourselves. I have found help in the Scriptures in raising children, in assuming my role as a woman, in arranging the priorities of my life. The Book of Proverbs is full of pithy little bits of wisdom; the Books of Peter deal with living the Christian life; James speaks to me about careless talk; the great principles of sin and redemption are clearly spelled out in Romans. These are available to me if only I read them. In the profusion of modern translations no one can claim that the language is obscure. The person who is serious about his relationship with God; who is serious about wanting to come closer to the person and purpose of Jesus; who is serious about knowing the power of God's Spirit in the world—this person must surely yearn for what comes to him through the incredible message of the Holy Scriptures. I sometimes trap myself into thinking that daily Bible reading is a very important duty instead of thinking of it as nourishment for my underdeveloped soul. It is a delight to discover what God would teach me through His Word.

There are many excellent guides to Bible study, and it isn't difficult to find one that fits the need. I can't resist adding an amateur's guide, for I suppose most of us are amateurs; and there are some helps that have been useful to me. It doesn't matter too much whose commentary or study guide you use as long as you check out the author in regard to his view of Scripture as authority. I say this because I have the reasonably simple view that God's Word is just that, and I have decided to accept all the Scriptures as having authority. I say this because I have the reasonably simple view that God's Word is just that, and I have decided to accept all Scriptures as having authority.[1]

It is important to study and read the Bible at whatever level is comfortable. I had read Paul's letters many times before I did research into Paul's life. An overly ambitious study program will often mean that you quit in the middle. There are some books of the Bible that I have read many times by now, but each time I find a new understanding, a new approach, a special verse that I had never noticed before. The material in the Bible is very durable, which is part of its continuing charm, and each time I read it I have a fresh perspective, for my understanding is always changing. In taking an art course this past year I was given a set of questions to ask about a work of art. The questions seemed interesting and with a little transposing I used these questions in some recent Bible study. What is the style of writing? Who wrote it, to whom was it written, and why was it written? Is it similar to anything else in the Bible? Why should I read it? What does it say to my own life?

In using this approach and any other that had appeal for me, I have read almost all of both the Old and New Testaments. Some of it has been hard going; I think the Old Testament is particularly difficult to understand, but it is worth the effort. There is something marvelously compelling about it, and after reading for awhile in the New Testament, I feel the need to expose myself once again to the passages in which Yahweh reveals Himself to His people. This is the God of Abraham, the

---

1. Perhaps this is said more clearly in the Articles of Religion, *Book of Common Prayer*: "Holy Scripture containeth all things necessary to salvation; so that whatsoever is not read therein, nor may be proved thereby, is not to be required of any man, that it should be believed as an article of the Faith, or be thought requisite or necessary to salvation. In the name of the Holy Scripture we do understand those canonical Books of the Old and New Testament, of whose authority was never any doubt in the Church."

God of Isaac, the God of Jacob. The Old Testament is dominated by Him, by God the Father, the Creator, the Just and Holy One; the New Testament speaks of the Son, God in human flesh, suffering, dying, and rising to newness of life. Taken together, the two Testaments are the most exciting reading in the world.

But the Bible is for living as well as reading; the Scriptures are for the eternal and for the now. The great principles laid out in the books of the Bible are as true today as they were a century ago. They are as valid for me as they were for Augustine. Paul writes to Corinth, but he writes to me as well. All the richness of the Scriptures are mine in a very personal way, but I need a certain approach to reading the Bible to get the most out of what I read. I believe that the Bible speaks to me most clearly when I open myself to it with no reservations, no disbeliefs, no sneers, no superiorities. I would be less than truthful if I didn't say that there are some passages my modern mind balks at accepting, but I have been helped by a talk I heard not long ago. Joe Blinco, a gifted Bible teacher who has been a member of the Billy Graham team, put it this way. In speaking of things that were difficult to swallow in the Bible he said this, "When you sit down to enjoy a fish dinner, you don't shove the meat aside in order to choke on the bones. Of course not! You carefully put aside the bones in order to enjoy the fish itself. Read the Bible with a bone-pile to one side, but don't throw away the good part." This is practical advice, and I have taken it. Although I have a good-sized bone pile, I am receiving the nourishment for which I had hoped.

I am the vine, you are the branches. He who
abides in me, and I in him, he it is that bears
much fruit, for apart from me you can do
nothing.

John 15:5 (RSV)

CHAPTER 8

CHAPTER 8

CREATED AND CREATIVE

I have always been a person with a creative bent, but until I came face to face with the reality of the Creator God, I didn't know what to do with the forces I felt bubbling inside. I didn't feel that I had any great talents, but in becoming a real part of creation through a relationship with the One who created everything, I was freed to be both created and creative.

I began my college career majoring in Costume Design, but the first art course that I took convinced me that whatever artistic talent was, I didn't have it. I struggled on in the Art Department for two more semesters, but I was so afraid of failure in a project that I couldn't work with freedom and originality. My grades were only average and I couldn't stand the thought of mediocrity, so I transferred to the Comparative Literature Department. It was a relief to escape the pressure of creative effort and to simply enjoy reading and studying some of the best writing in the world, but I never lost the sense of longing to produce something beautiful and original.

One of the qualities that attracted me to Bob was his talent for architectural design; I sensed that he had the spark that I lacked. Throughout his career as a designer and builder of homes I have participated vicariously and shared the pleasure of his creation with him. I took pride in his accomplishment, and I was happy that his talent was so materially rewarding. I sometimes wished during the early years of our marriage that I had more to show for my own creative efforts, but the fact was, cooking was my major creative outlet and we ate up my masterpieces three times a day. Our home was lovely, but I felt that it reflected Bob's talent and not mine. With children it seldom looked like *House Beautiful* anyway; even without the clutter, I had long since decided that dust would defeat me in the end. I had a maid, but I wasn't an effective homemaker.

Although I had some free time, I never seemed to do much with it. I wasn't creating anything; I was still too afraid of failing or looking foolish. If I couldn't have a one-woman show at the local museum, I didn't want to paint; why write a book that nobody would read? I had forgotten my piano lessons; I was too old for modern dance and too young for china painting. I didn't want to do anything in bad taste, so I dare nothing and accomplished very little. The coming into my life of the Holy Spirit of God changed all that. In these past four years I have opened like a flower to the real possibilities of my own talents and unique abilities. Creativity is by no means limited to the arts; I have discovered that there is such a thing as creative living.

My greatest opportunity for creative activity was right under my nose all along, but it took the new vision that God gave me to really see it. I'm talking about my children and the understanding I now have of the vast difference between physical motherhood and spiritual motherhood. I was a fairly competent mother—I saw to manners and visits to the dentist and proper diet—but until I saw human beings as spiritual beings I could not offer my youngsters real guidance, sculpturing of the soul. Being a spiritual mother is to enter into the total aspect of creation itself, the ever-changing complexity of relationship. It is God's grace that sustains me in this difficult venture. Mothering is a lot of work; it takes time and patience; it is often years before the results emerge. Worse, I know that I'm making mistakes. I am comforted, however, by the thought that now God can help me with those errors of judgment that I make. One of the things for which I am most grateful is that Christ became real for Bob and me before it was too late, as far as our children were concerned.

Soon after Bob and I began to live as Christians we saw our responsibility for communicating the faith to our two boys, who were then six and eight. I assumed the duty of reading *Little Visits with God* with them each night and having a time of prayer out loud. I'm afraid I was looking for instant conversion and precocious religious understanding, and there were times when I was very angry over their lack of respect for a solemn occasion. Some of the Bible stories bored them and occasionally they giggled during prayers. My younger son developed his own prayer— "Thank you, God, for everything and everything else amen." It was certainly all-inclusive but not very specific. We have continued prayers, though, and now the boys sometimes read to their little sister some of the stories they like best in their children's Bible. I have gotten over my compulsiveness and realize that there is God's good time for everything. Robin, who will be twelve this year, is taking instruction in Confirmation class at our church, and the seriousness of his study in preparation for the classes is a satisfaction to me. He knows who Jesus is, he accepts Him as his Savior, and he is eager to acknowledge Him as such publicly, in the manner provided in the Episcopal Church.

As a mother, I am an artist, altering nature, molding, taking liberties, making choices. Not only that, I have three works of art in process at the same time, each of them at a different stage with totally different needs. I love my children and I nurture them, but my biggest job is to prepare them to leave me. There is a big world beyond our home, and within the confines of the environment I create for them, and I am trying to give them the faith and the strength to face the best and the worst that life has to offer. I cannot become a woman who lays up her treasure in her children, cherishing them too much. Because I am a mother I can feel the strong pull of the mother-child relationship, but I am also poised at the place of being both mother and child. Too much mother love produces smothered children who never grow up and disappointed women who are no longer needed in the way that they want to be needed.

The primary relationship in the home should be that of husband and wife—"the two shall become one" (Ephesians 5:31), as Paul says. The greatest security for the child growing into adulthood is the knowledge that his parents love and respect each other, and the only sure way that each parent is able to do this is through the grace of God. To seek first the kingdom of God and His righteousness, insures a husband-wife relationship patterned after God's eternal purpose. To seek first the kingdom of God and His righteousness—that is to insure that children will grow strong, knowing and loving the Author of all knowledge and all love.

The creativity of women is not limited to those who are mothers. Most women, particularly those who are alive to God, have the instinct to make life lovelier; to create happiness—a little place of warmth in a cold world. The instinct is sometime buried deep and it may not come to the surface readily; but if we are freed by God to be what He intended, each of us is creative, whatever the circumstances. The world is deficient in love, and the Christian should be God's agent to offer His love.

I know a woman who is nearly seventy years old. She never had any children of her own; her husband, whom she married late in life, died some years ago. She is financially independent, but she has the responsibility of making a home for her mother and her sister. Taken at face value these circumstances do not seem very exciting, but add to them the fact that she loves to teach children, and you begin to see what her life is really like.

She has taught in elementary schools for at least four decades; when one school system retired her at the mandatory age, she found a smaller school system that needed her. Each year's children are "her children" for that year, and she is very much interested in them as individuals. For Christmas this year she sewed a shirt for each boy and a dress for each girl. She worked arithmetic into the project by letting the children measure each other. She lavishes love as well as learning. Many of "her children" have never before met an adult who felt that they were important, who recognized them as having value.

In the past year I have found an opportunity to combine my love of art and my concern for people. One morning a week I am what is called a "picture lady" in the local public schools. This means that I take reproductions of art masterpieces to classrooms and, together, the children and I respond to the things that we see in each painting. It is a fun time for me and the children love it; besides the art, it is a chance for some of them to feel important, because I tell them at the beginning that there are no wrong answers, only different ones. As important as information about art is, the main feeling that I want to give these children of varying ability and background is the feeling that their ideas are of value to me. It isn't much but it is a small offering of God's love, though the name of God is never mentioned. If God is really involved in a personal way with His world, then His Spirit permeates the whole of life. There are no religious situations for me as a Christian; my life cannot be divided into compartments, arranged and indexed according to religious significance. I need to be God's person wherever I am. Whatever the occupation of the Christian it fits into the whole of God's creative effort, and I do even my dullest tasks in the presence of God Almighty.

The use of talents is bound up with the use of time, and in this area I cannot beg off on the grounds that I don't have as much as any other person. There are twenty-four hours in every person's day. God has begun showing me something about the creative use of time. As a baby, our little girl had to be fed every three hours, morning and night, and I hated those interruptions in my sleep. In the letter to the Ephesians Paul speaks of "making the most of time" and I decided that perhaps he was talking about just such a situation as mine. I began using the 2:00 A.M. feeding as a quiet time of prayer, and believe me, it is quiet at that hour. During the period of time that I had night feedings my prayer life was strong, and I know that I interceded for more people than I have since, now that I'm sleeping all night. Have you ever been trapped in a doctor's office with old magazines? Use the time to pray and you may find that the time passes quickly and that you have actually enjoyed the delay. Creative use of time is not so much getting things done as what happens to you in the doing.

Each of us possesses something in the material sense, although some of us are admittedly more fortunate than others. As with our talents and our time, money is the gift of God even though we may have done much of the work acquiring it. Many Christians feel guilty about having possessions; one minister I know feels guilty about the amount of salary that he receives. We all live in the material world and we cannot escape the problem of possessions; feeling guilty does not really help. The Hebrew custom of offering the first tenth of the crop to God comes down to us as tithing. There are many questions that Christians today ask about tithing. Do you figure the tenth before or after taxes? Where should the tithe go? For me such questions miss the point. I believe that everything belongs to God and that He has dominion over all that I have. Bob and I are His stewards, and He cares very much how we spend the other nine-tenths of our income.

This was brought home to me several years ago. Bob came home one evening and told me of a boy we knew who was in jail on charges of vandalism. We knew the family situation—the father had died when the boy was quite small and he felt that the world was very unfair to him. He was now in serious trouble, and as Bob talked, I felt sympathy for the boy and his mother. But when Bob went on to say that he had signed his bail bond as surety for his appearance in court, I was horrified at the sum of money involved. It didn't seem fair for us to be responsible for that boy. Then I thought, "Nancy, there you go again, thinking that it all belongs to you. You have to trust God in this." I then offered up my reluctance and was given a sense of peace about the outcome. I'm happy to say that the bond was not forfeited and that the boy's rehabilitation began with a suspended sentence. He did get another chance, but the nice ending is not really the point. I had to learn to be generous if this was what God wanted from me in that situation.

It seems that creativity involves far more for me now. To bake a pie for a bereaved family, to visit a tiresome old woman who repeats herself, to offer a smile to a timid child—this is holy work and part of God's creation. I still regret that I cannot play the piano, but I sing in church. I still would like to paint like Renoir, but I know I won't. But it's all right; God has freed me to see beauty all around and I need only be a grateful appreciator of all that He has created.

O Eternal Trinity! O Godhead! Thou art a
deep Sea, into which the deeper I enter the
more I find, and the more I find the more I
seek.

St. Catherine of Sienna

CHAPTER 9

THE REAL AND ONLY LIFE

What is the Christian life really like? What does it look like? What does it feel like? I have to say that it is not the way I expected it to be. Four years ago I shared some of the same feelings that the world has about Christianity.

The feeling that many people have about Christians is that we are vaguely medieval, or at best mid-nineteenth century. We don't seem to speak the language of the day; our ideas seem out of date. Quite frankly, a lot of us do not communicate effectively with the people "out there"—and we have little to do with them. Some of us who are Christians give outsiders the feeling that Christianity is simply the bulwark of good manners, acceptable morals and polite piety. They quite rightly fault us for our assumption that we are better than anyone else.

The fact is, the mature Christian is the one who knows, and all too bitterly, that he is a sinner, a wrong-doer, totally without hope of perfection in this present life. Human nature is flawed and not one of us can escape the condition of being human. My humanity will inevitably lead me into trouble and conflict, no matter how fine my intentions are. In our own time we have seen many sincere efforts to improve mankind socially, economically, educationally. But what makes us so sure that we can change the human heart? If it were possible, surely it would have been done by now, for ours is not the first generation to care what happens to people. For if man could create for himself a world of love and peace, we would not now have the fragmented, problem-ridden society we see around us. We face today exactly the same problem as those who came before us—the perversity of the human spirit.

Human nature is a fatal disease; death most certainly will come to each of us. That which is of the earth must die, and that means me. Where, then, is hope? I find it in the acceptance of the very different nature of Jesus who was both God and man, spirit and flesh. He died, but He rose again. He is the *new* Man and the life lived in Christ is the new life. It is, for me, the only life worth living.

A person does not find himself by moving from place to place, wife to wife, job to job. He finds himself by definition, in the context of the present moment. What is man looking for, if not for an understanding of himself—the answer to the question of identity? For me the point of definition is to be found in the perfected God-man relationship as Jesus lived it. And the Christian life as I have found it these past four years is a life of acting on the knowledge of Christ Himself. There are certain things that I have come to understand about my relationship to God in Jesus Christ—these are the things this book is about. This is my knowledge of Christ. I hope in God's grace that this knowledge will increase, but my part is to act on what I already know.

Our reactions and responses tell the most about us, what we are really like, so God begins His new creation in the most basic relationships of our lives. In the years before my conversion I had managed to mess up every major relationship of my life. My problem was my total self-centeredness. Self-centeredness just won't work unless you control the universe, and the limitations of the flesh make it impossible to satisfy the ever-increasing needs of the self. Self will demand its due and self must begin to die before the new life can be ascendant.

One of the first things God showed me about myself was that my sensitivity and hurt feelings were sins. I had always felt picked on by other people and my wounded feelings were proof of the persecution. I began to see this as a monstrous form of self-center-edness. God let me see how unfair I was being to others. I was sure they were going to hurt me and in a funny way I made sure they did! Psychology can better define this, but I understood the reaction well enough to know that I had to give up this sensi-tivity. With God's help I began to do so; and although I still feel a stab occasionally, most of the time I am able to accept criticism as either just or unjust, to be acted on or rejected.

I became aware of the burden I had placed on my husband. Poor Bob! I had made him the custodian of my happiness; and if he could supply my enormous need for love, praise, admira-tion, and support, then all was well. If he was not able to do so, then he was a disappointment and I became depressed. It was absurd for me to expect someone else to make me happy or un-happy; I needed to stand on my own two feet and be responsible for my own well-being. I began to change in this area before Bob and I began our life together in Christ, but he remembers the time I began freeing him from his burden. He didn't know why I was doing it, but he felt a sense of relief. Our relationship is both freer and closer than it ever was before; we are no longer engaged in the struggle of two self-centered wills.

My children had been extensions of my ego, but now I have to allow them the freedom to be themselves. Because I had ex-celled as a student, it was in this area that I had the greatest difficulty with my school-age children. When my older son went to the first grade I practically went with him. An "A" paper made it a good day for mother and son; a "C" was a disgrace for us both. I was putting on the pressure until it became clear to me that my son's mind was not my mind all over again, and that win, lose, or draw, he was the one who made the grades. I'm still interested, delighted with good work, concerned with less than good work, but the pressure is off and my son knows it. It was amazing how much his work improved when I didn't try to do it for him. Robin is Robin; Greg is Greg; Jennifer is Jennifer— not one of them is like the other. It is the richness of the differences in them that makes being their mother so much fun.

People seem different to me now; I'm not afraid of them anymore. I by no means like all of them, nor do I enjoy each and every one of them; but I see them now, not as enemies to be hidden from, but as fellow-pilgrims. Some of them are lost; some of them are forging ahead so I may follow them. My friends in Christ are dear and special to me, for we are bonded together in Him; but in some way God gives me a concern for those who aren't my friends, those who do not seem lovable to me at all. He has opened me to people in a way that I never dreamed possible, and in doing so, He has filled my life with blessings for which I never thought to ask.

I used to think that if I really gave myself to God He would mold me into a neat little package labeled "Christian." What really happened when I decided to chance it, to commit myself anyway, was that God the great Creator began to free me to be more myself than I had ever been before. This is true for many Christians and perhaps accounts for the diversity of opinion and responsive action to point of view in the Christian Church. Some feel the impact of social problems; others devote themselves to spreading the good news about Jesus Christ; and there are those who must explore the meaning of life in God's physical world. The magnitude of God's grace can encompass many different personalities, ideas, doctrines, and denominations so long as Jesus the Christ is the center of the circle. My experience of the reality of God is not identical to anyone else's experience, and although the hallmark of the Christian seems to be a quality of life produced by the Holy Spirit, no two lives are ever alike.

My husband and I share the same faith, but our insights are sometimes very different. He has a wonderfully uncomplicated understanding of the Christian life, and he finds this understanding in examples very close to home. In speaking at conferences Bob sometimes closes with a little story about our daughter Jennifer. One night, when she was about eighteen months old, Bob was putting her to bed. She was restless and she didn't want her daddy to leave the room. He soothed her and turned to leave. She popped up in her crib and said, "Da-da?" Bob looked at her, so tiny, so beautiful, so helpless, and he was overwhelmed with love for that little child. She couldn't completely understand him because she was such a little baby; she couldn't really speak his language. She couldn't do much for Bob, but he loved her with all his heart. He said, "Jennifer, don't be afraid. I won't ever leave you. Why, I'd even die for you!" And in that moment, Bob realized for the first time the real meaning of God's love for him. And he saw that as he wanted Jennifer to believe him and trust him, so God wanted him to respond to this love unto death by simply accepting the great gift offered him.

It is a mystery, but it seems that the Cross is the point at which all lines of history converge. It is both the beginning and the end of all creation. In practical terms there is no blessed forgiveness, no plea for mercy, no hope of newness of life without the completed sacrifice of God's Son. I don't like to think of what it cost God to buy me back, to give me a new life, but it is only when I come onto the most sacred ground of the Cross of Christ that I know my salvation. I am precious in God's sight; me, with all my problems, my sins, my few virtues. I am a person with a price on my head, for God exchanged the life of His Son for that of a mixed-up creature like me.

What God in Jesus Christ offers us is life; to live a life full of things, people, places, ideas, love—the full circle of all that it means to be alive. This life includes the joy of understanding, the pain of loss, suffering, unmeasured love, times of darkness. The Christian life as it has unfolded for me has not been a narrow, artificial attempt at early sainthood. It has been full, abundant, overflowing; above all, it has never been boring. I do not know where He is leading me, but leading me He is, and that is the real and only life.

Nancy Peerman played a succession of games—
she became, in rapid and never-ending
succession, the capable mother—perfect wife—
elegant hostess—superficial socialite. Her efforts
to find reality were regularly bolstered by
Tranquilizers and high-balls. Beneath the proper
and apparently impenetrable veneer, though,
was the scared-little-girl which only she knew
was there.

This is the story of Nancy Peerman's search for
herself, and for reality. How she found both of
these is an almost classic story, written with the
simplicity and directness which characterizes
all really good writing.

Keith Miller says of this book,
"This is an authentic Christian witness and I
believe it will help thousands of people to find
new direction toward a life which is 'really real'."